The Wild Woods Edge

The Wild Woods Edge

poems by

Bart Price

Illustrated by
Joseph Price

aquiet press

The Wild Woods Edge
Copyright © 2013 by Bart C. Price
Published by aquiet press, Nashville, Tennessee

All rights reserved. No part of this book may be reproduced in any form or by any electronic or mechanical means, including information storage and retrieval systems, without written permission from the author.

ISBN 978-0-9888868-0-3

Cover design by Bart Price

Printed in the United States of America

To
Bud and Mama

Contents

Preface 1

I

Survival of the Fittest   *9*
Imagination   *11*
I Am a Fighter   *12*
The Picnic   *13*
Dreams   *15*
I Saw U   *16*
Rejection Letters   *18*
Mixed Drink   *19*
Heroic Lives   *20*
Showing Up   *21*
New Year's Day   *22*
Last Love   *23*
In the Garden   *25*
If There Be Ought   *27*
Saints   *28*
A Task   *29*
Before I Was Born   *30*
Profile   *32*
Allure   *34*
Texting   *35*
Two Lights   *36*

II

The Beloved   *43*
Life Here   *45*
Just Yesterday   *46*

Millinocket in August   *47*
Leaves in the Grass   *48*
Living   *49*
Contemplation   *50*
Hunger   *52*
A Gift   *53*
Wild or Tame?   *55*
It Was All a Blurrrrrrrrr   *56*
In the Park   *57*
An Encounter   *58*
Pain and Beauty   *59*
Age of Exploration   *61*
Things Foreign   *62*
Prayer upon a Wall   *63*
For Ezra   *64*
Wrapper in the Wild   *65*
Upon Meeting a Certain Woman   *66*
The Place We Grew Up In   *68*
Gibberish   *69*

III

I Once Met a Soul   *75*
To My Love   *76*
The Garbage Man   *77*
Mystery   *79*
Agnosticism   *80*
The Final Hour   *81*
Freedom   *83*
When I Soared Above the Clouds   *84*
What the Sea Saw   *85*
Love in the Wild   *86*
Like unto These   *88*
Naming Things   *89*

Improv *90*
Love's Approach *91*
Holiness *92*
Anticipation *93*
Before Dusk *95*
Mystical Union *97*
Compatibility *98*
Balance Sheets *99*
Shadows *100*
Bright-eyed and Young *102*
First and Last Things *103*
When I Arrived in Heaven *104*

About the Author *107*

Preface

It was my intention, in writing this volume over the past year, to create a body of work to be enjoyed by all who come to it. Since writing is not merely a matter of communication, but also of self-discovery, I can say I have learned a great deal about myself in writing this book. Perhaps you will learn at least a little about yourself in reading it. Such is my hope and expectation, anyway. After all, I believe it is within the community of the Body as a whole, in the exchange among ourselves and others, that we learn about ourselves and the world around us. More precisely, I believe, we learn most about life while in a position of admiration, when our souls stand ajar, you might say; by that, I mean when we look outward rather than inward, when we look at a forested mountain glade or person or some other grandeur of God with deep appreciation, when we observe with a loving regard rather than with an analytical eye – it is then that we allow the essence and beauty of such a thing or person to wash over us like grace; it is then that we are open to learning most about life, I believe.

As for the poems in this collection, they are the fruit of looking at life in this way, or trying to at least. For this reason, I say I hope the fruit is good. Indeed, the palate cannot take too much sourness, or blandness, or bad texture, or emotionalism, or esotericism even. As regards to this latter point, I allude back to my first statement: It does no good for writers of poetry to isolate themselves from the Body. If they do, they risk cutting off the means by which they come to know themselves and the world around them, as well as the means by which the members of the Body come to know these things. And, as I have already faintly implied, this arrival at greater knowledge of life is one of the rewards – if not one of the purposes – of poetry, or of any writing for that matter.

If I may speak further on the matter of poetry's purpose, I must first say that much poetry in the past few decades seems to come from, I hate to admit, the most hopeless among us, as if such poets were hoping, or hoping against hope, to ensnare us in their hopelessness. Novelist Flannery O'Connor once said that people without hope do not write novels. Perhaps not, but they do write poetry. And with them I disagree, for I believe poets should strive to communicate a sense of beauty, or delight. Such is easy to forget, and authors would do well to remember this point. Take the novel, for instance. How many novels are written with only an eye toward telling a good story? By that, I mean ensuring good content. Indeed, good storytelling is all fine and good, but what if more authors took things a step further and not only related a good story but went about telling it in language that would put a wide smile on the reader's face, a smile expressing wonder at how something was put into language so elegantly? Certainly, doing so would make all within proximity of such a reader wonder what they were missing out on and whether they, too, should have picked up that novel in the airport bookstore before heading to terminal B. Indeed, it is a matter of the *what* and the *how* – what is told and how it is told. Likewise, I believe good poetry cannot live long without the beauty of the *how*.

But let me go back just for a moment to my point on esotericism: It seems much modern poetry falls prey to this trap. With authors of such poetry isolating themselves in ivory towers, it is no wonder that modern culture embraces poetry much less now than, say, during the nineteenth century or even the first half of the twentieth century. I know there are other factors at play, and I also know I am censuring a great deal of poetry. However, to sum up my point quickly and succinctly, I give you an example of a painter who once told me he spent a third of his day – half, if you consider that a third of it is spent sleeping – for an entire year painting a gigantic oak tree. Granted, it was the grandest of trees I had ever seen put to canvas, so detailed one could see the outlines of bark throughout the trunk and boughs, and the veins coursing through every singular leaf, not to mention the individual blades of grass springing up under the old oak's shade. Certainly, it was a masterpiece of skill. Yet how many would buy such a piece of work, given the choice between it and a painting of a less detailed, yet more diverse, landscape?

If I have been overly critical here, please forgive me. Really, I am simply trying to say if poetry is ever to become recognized again in modern culture, its expression should communicate a sense of delight, as I have said. At the same time, it should be able to inspire and enlarge the hearts and minds of all persons, provided they have open minds and hearts. And finally, poetry should exude a kind of mystery, or wildness, you might say, the depths of which cannot fully be plumbed. I have found, in writing as in life, the phosphorescence, the inchoate mystery of something, is found not in veering recklessly to the left or the right, but in the middle, at the mean of two extremes. Having said this, then, it is my hope this volume as a whole contains the kind of mystery and delight that gives the poems in it, in their totality of force, a living, breathing life that touches all who come to them.

– Bart Price, *St. Augustine*
January 2013

I

It is not down in any map; true places never are.

— *Moby-Dick,* Herman Melville

The woods beyond the yard sang with the sultry sound of insects stinging the air. A crescent moon lit up the surrounding forest and glimmered on the lake, making the ripples visible on the water. There was a light breeze and I sat with my legs crossed, listening to the gulping sound the water made as it sloshed gently against the dock. The night air was fresh and dry, the sky full of stars. I recalled the song "Twinkle, Twinkle, Little Star," and for probably the hundredth time since I had been living there, I renewed once more in my mind the truth in that title – the stars, all of them, seeming to twinkle, one after another, across the whole of the dark, cloudless sky. The insects seemed louder than usual, so clear and transparent was the air. A fish jumped about a half mile across the lake, sending water shaking and spitting. The stillness of the night made it sound as if the fish had been right next to the dock. A fishy smell, which seemed pleasant due to its naturalness in the wild, like the smell of a horse or dog, wafted on the billows of wind from time to time.

Survival of the Fittest

Each tree is a family,
    every leaf, a narration,
each bough, a person,
    every ring, a generation.

We mavericks crave unity
    yet shun any control.
Allowing nature to beget, we all go astray,
    each and every soul.

But in another time to come
    the fittest will survive.
Allowing love to beget, they won't go astray,
    no longer will divide.

To what this generation shall be likened
    the rings of time will show.
It can take ages for things to come together,
    like a sequoia tree or lava flow.

Imagination

Imagination is a country road that runs through the city,
creating a thing unforeseen
and that does not seem to belong

                              – though just seem,

for the city needs a country road,
lined with thorny bushes, tangled trees and wend-
ing weeds.

I Am a Fighter

I am a fighter, not a lover,
a boxer with tender conscience,
a devil converted.

I am a fighter, not a lover,
a red-blooded male with deft control,
a knight in tattered armor.

'I am a lover, not a fighter'
– don't let this soft saying seduce;
'tis not nobler to be a lover.

But a fighter?

I am a fighter, not a lover.

The Picnic

I wonder what it was like –
I mean the picnic?

What was talked about on their way up the mountain –
their love of the sea?
Typee or Happar?
Roger Malvin's burial?

When it was almost time to eat, did he who would be
a future diplomat sit quietly,
penetrating the souls of those around him,
while the future custom inspector for the City of New York escaped
into a savage world?

Perhaps they spoke of common things – tending horses, that
Sir Robert Peel fell off his, that
a kitchen clock, excellent at timekeeping, was selling at $1.50, that
a fellow named Levi Strauss had invented a pair of jeans.

Did they, with interest, engage in conversation
when asked about how they and their wives, who sat beside them
in Victorian dresses and side-lace boots, liked the Berkshires?

Were they about to eat fish
before they saw the dark thundercloud approaching,
and did they allow the others to squeeze in tight
around the blanket spread upon the grass?

Or were they each like the Mulungu god, going off by themselves,
smoking cigars and sipping brandy
and, when the rainstorm finally struck,

taking cover under a rocky ledge,
their hearts beating
in each's ribs   *whence come you?*

And was it there
that they opened their abstract hearts,
discussed the loss of their fathers, time and eternity, blackness,
beauty?

Was it then that their faces alighted like fireflies in August,
that they – each almost alone in their generation – knew for certain
that immortality existed?

And was it then, at that moment,
that germinal seeds were dropped into their souls,
that sparks flew out of the common breeze,
that, at the time unbeknownst to it,
set the whole snow-hilled, seven-gabled world
aflame?

Dreams

Some dream of expensive clothes,
others, of a house along the New England coast,
others, of a chalet in the Rocky Mountains,
a six-figure salary,
a more decked-out car,
a wider flat-screen TV,
faster Internet service,
more RAM,
an iPhone
(so as to log onto Facebook every few minutes while having a romantic evening with their lover).

Yet others
dream of a blanket at night
under a warm banana moon,
devouring, with the earnings left over from the temp. job,
a cold ham & cheese.

I Saw U

You: Large antlers and muscular
legs, standing in the sun atop
White Cap Mountain, grazing on
wild blueberries. Me: Under
the shade of a small birch tree,
too shy to look back when you looked
at me. If by chance you read this,
I'll be on White Cap in autumn,
near the wild blueberries; would love
to get to know you

Rejection Letters

Those I have asked to dinner
or to coffee
or to the movies, as well as I,
have either been publishers or authors –
some new to the company, or the art,
others not.
Nevertheless, rejection letters are our lot,
and we come to understand them.
Only authors who have never worked at
a Simon & Schuster, HarperCollins or Random House
or have not been employed there long,
do not understand them
and take them to heart
and brood over them
and hesitate to submit
another piece of art.

But as for me, I frame them,
for they are reminders of the progress I am making
toward breaking
into print.

Mixed Drink

Give me rum or Coke,
but don't give me rum and Coke.

Give me scotch,
but don't dare put it on the rocks.

But truth and love?

I'll take that
– but never truth or love.

Heroic Lives
(A lyric written posthumously)

We lived heroic lives, we did.
We did not die for the faith,
      yet we did die for it,
                      white-blooded death,
it was.

Relatively alone in a place called home,
browns, blacks, blondes, reds among seas of white –
not much different than others of our generation,
the difference being objectification
of truth.

But it was the abiding in that clean, fresh stream,
an alcove running through a narrow gorge,
like through a needle's eye,
trees towering into the sky
on either side,
that saved us, turns out,
becoming a rippling rivulet to the sea, dark-light pure as we were.

We lived heroic lives, we did.
We did not die for the faith,
      yet we did die for it,
                      white-blooded death,
it was.

Showing Up

Ninety-nine percent of success is simply
showing up

– on time –

to work,
to a date,
to a friend's need,
to a wife's need,
to a husband's need,
to a child's need,
to help someone in need,
to the YMCA,
to pray,
for your wedding night,
for last rites....

New Year's Day

It was New Year's Day
at ten o'clock in the morning.
I was still lying in bed,
my head filled with wine
and a dumbbell in my stomach,
not wanting to get up.
It was cold inside
and I longed for warmth.

I thought about what resolution
I wanted to make this year:
to be a better person,
more temperate, more loving,
kinder, humbler.

But I knew in a month's time
I will have fallen short of this –
of such a daunting goal – which
for some mysterious reason
I dreamt to attain.

Only years later did I realize
I was not alone,
that others too, deep down,
long for New Year's Day to be every month,
if not every week (and why can't it be, if it is the way
we choose?), so that having fallen short of our vows
we once again might have
our slates wiped clean,
a fresh start on life
and a greater purpose in living.

Last Love

This was not my first infatuation
but my last love –
having had five before.

With an intellect sharp,
a beauty strong and an eager heart,
it seemed certainty this infatuation,
this time, could become love.
No chance of hurt,
no risk of wound –
it seemed the heart was safe with this one,
who would never reject at a later hour,

    never.

In the Garden

"Mr. Yanga," I said,
standing in the wide shade of a peach tree,
narrowing my eyes as I looked at its plump fruit hanging
from the boughs.

"Yes," he said, straining to look up at me,
the sun in his face,
the sweat on his brow,
his bare knees in the dirt,
having pulled weeds all morning in the garden.

Gazing up at the magical fruit,
I said, "Keats once wrote,
'Beauty is truth, truth beauty – that is all ye know on earth,
and all ye need to know,'

and I tend to agree with him."
I looked down at Mr. Yanga, my neighbor,
his eyes still fixed on mine.

I continued, my hands in my pockets,
gazing at the mystical boughs:
"I've discovered I love what is true and
beautiful and good in this world."

I looked down at Mr. Yanga again,
eager for his reaction,
poet and lover of the Romantics he was.

Without hesitation, his wrinkled eyes widened
against the light

and a soft smile burst from his face,
brighter and certainly more tender
than the sun at this present noon,
as if all the years of labor had made it so.

"That's good," he said
simply,

"but that's not love."

If There Be Ought

If a single man be as happy as a lark,
   should he marry?

If his companion be as solitary as an aardvark,
   should she marry?

    "Aye, they should," said the red kite,
      "if they're in love."

      "But," interjected the bee, "ought there be ought, too?"

    "Yes, there must be ought," the kite agreed.

        "That's right," the pigeon chimed. "Where there are
          feelings there's not always ought."

      "Well said, pigeon," said the bee. "Ought is
        love's confirmation."

Saints

Saints of God are rebels

– to the world –

red-lipped,
foot-firm,
glass-full,
door-open,
nail-kind,
an independent mind,
unbrackished and defying

– like wild salmon
swimming upstream.

A Task

Out of ignorance boredom exists,
like evil, or dark matter:
the absence of.

From the cultivated field arises
alfalfa and sweet-smelling corn
and okra. Should I appreciate okra – I did not say like –
and Gertrude Stein's poetry?

Manifest destiny in modernity
says grow old in sameness.
But is there really such a thing as the average Joe?
Or is he common
because he's allowed himself to be so?

Since truth leads to truth, as road leads to road,
perhaps,
perhaps.

After all,
we seem to have infinite potential to grow.

To appreciate what is real, wherever it may be –
is that a task too tall to topple?

Before I Was Born

Before I was born I lived a life of adversity.
There was not one path laid out for me,
but infinite paths,
so I sincerely chose a pagan one.

And by struggle and strife enough,
whatever other earnest diversions I took,
in time God knew he would make me holy
by hook or by crook.

Profile

Looking for a REAL DRAKE who takes
his life serious, who is smart, has colorful
plumes, is well educated and still
humble. Me? I am 30-something
duck from Chicago, spent my
days at a retention pond next to
an ad agency in downtown
and recently moved to South. There are
three things I love about living
in South; Beautiful weather, People and Collard
green (I don't eat them, but I like
to smell them). And there are three things I hate
about living in South; Steamy summer
weather, Awful department store roofs
and I can't seem to find drake
that fits my "standard". I have two Masters
degrees (one in ornithology
and the other in zoology)
and my job requires me to be
trendy and sassy. I dress
well, so I will let you count my shoes
ONLY if you want. I am petite,
have long dark feathers and skinny
figure. I eat all kind of food
and studied possum cuisine as well. I go
to the church steeple on Sundays
and I think nothing prettier than church
organ sound. I waddle to Brahms nice
and I cut my own feathers. I love to quack
and also love to make others quack.
I am also very focused on my

career and always trying to learn new
things as much I can. I have been working
very hard since I flew to
Chicago in 2007.
And now, I feel like I am ready to find
my behalf. Please ONLY contact
me if you are seriously interested
to get to know me. I do not want
casual encounters at this time.

Allure

perfume ocean
tender
elegant
body swaying
dipping
the allure!
the allure!

being swept
deferring
feeling his arms
the allure!
feeling the rhythm
the allure!

chests pounding
the allure!
eyes meeting
hearts facing
ah, the glow!
ah, the glow!

Texting

r u goin 2nite

                    hehe, i might
how bout u?

                    if i get sum new shoe
s

    k :)

Two Lights

Two climb upwards
on a mass transit to the top,
striking out ahead of the pack
in their long night's journey into day.
"*Verso l'alto!*" they say
(their mantra).

At the top they expect to meet the light,
which will point them home.
But to them unbeknown
there will be two lights – a crossroads –
both well-lit as far as they will see,
and attractive equally.

When the first gets to the top
(it doesn't take him long;
he is still strong)
he takes a right,
ignoring his brother's advice.
And it is not long
before he finds the path increasingly arduous
and begins to feel something is not right,
that he must have gone on
too far.

It can't be this far, he thinks,
while the feeling sets in that perhaps – no, it can't be,
yet maybe it is so – he is lost somehow.
His adrenaline rushing,
his heart beating faster,
he glances back toward the light

coming from the direction in which his brother had gone,
wondering if it was the way he, too,
should have taken.

For a moment, amidst his racing mind,
he imagines home.
But, he thinks,
he has gone too far to turn back now
even if death is a possibility.
His breathing shallower, his eyesight hazy,
and driven by fear, he continues on,
picking up the pace.

Then, only a short distance later,
he stops,
dizzy and faint;
he can go no farther.
In exhaustion he peers up
into the darkness,
seeing that the light he has been following –
what the loggerhead thought was the moonlight beckoning him on –
is a street lamp.

II

Well, I like to eat, sleep, drink, and be in love.
I like to work, read, learn, and understand life.

– from *Theme for English B,* Langston Hughes

I drove along the winding road that led out of town, climbing steadily through the lush, green mountains. My car skirted the edges of drop-offs that plunged deep into the canopy of trees, occasionally dipping into a valley before rising again to climb higher than before. The road was well-paved, but in some spots potholes had formed due to icing in winter. As I maneuvered around sheer rock-face bends in the road, the sun seemed to be engaged with me in a game of sorts. Every once in a while its pale, yellow gaze leapt out from behind one of the bends, bold and beaming, discovered and yet unabashedly standing its ground. I continued climbing higher and higher into a forest steadily becoming more remote. A squirrel sprinted out of the woods and across the road, as if trying to compete with me. It happened so fast and far enough ahead of my car I didn't need to brake. I wondered if such was a little game the squirrels played and we humans thought they just sometimes mindlessly darted out of the bushes. Perhaps they thrived off a challenge. Perhaps they were even happiest when challenged.

The Beloved

Where has my love gone!
To the sea she has gone!
Weeping for her sins
amid the black-tip fins!

Go get her and bring her back!
Go get her and bring her to my shack!
I will treat her wounds and wash her clean,
for her weeping will make her sheen!

Life Here

Slopes of steep mountains do I tread
to make way to the sea.
Why I climbed them in the first place
and how I had gotten this far inland, into the wild,
up and over those same mountains so effortlessly, it seems,
I do not know.

Yet is it the sea I desire
or is my desire, in the flesh, more for a sea of sorts?
For what life can be found in the wild, a lovely place!
Such is perhaps as it should be –
life here is best lived along the undulation
with a view of the sea.

Just Yesterday

Funny how a book I picked up
at Barnes & Noble three days ago
on the display rack at the front of the store –
you know, the one you see
right when you walk in and hear the sound
of intellect playing in the background? –
told me science has
once and for all
proven God does not exist.

Funny because just yesterday
I saw God coming out of Barnes & Noble
as I was going in
to get a cup of coffee after work and,
as I have a habit of doing these days, read
until it was time to go home – she a striking paradox of age and
dressed in a mysterious white unbroken from head to heel,
floating past the display, smiling
as if I were the only one.

And so today for the first time
in a long time, instead of going to Barnes & Noble,
I drove out to a secluded beach
awash with crabs and starfish and huge seashells,
the deep blue air smelling of brine, the breeze whispering
in my ear, like a seascape set to Chopin's Nocturne Opus 9,
No. 2, recalling how my discarding
that pale tome back onto the rack three days ago
seemed to have taken place in another life, or a dream.

Millinocket in August

Millinocket in August can feel like a winter's day,
as the wind strips the unsuspecting leaves from the birch trees
and the chimneys of the quaint New England homes
begin to gasp.

Ah, winter! – not far from the summer's heat and vigor.
Today I will make haste while I can, gathering up stores for
the summer's coming wrath, which can overtake the winter
just as quickly.

Leaves in the Grass

Did you ever notice then,
at that time and place
(and what appeared only to be time and place),
how clouds created emotion,
how one day was soft and another hard,
cold, uninteresting?

Did you ever notice, for instance, how cirrus clouds created
a sweet melancholy that gave life its flavor,
like suffering?

It was these soft, mellow days I loved best,
like a woman,

the autumn days of coolness and crispness,
when leaves in the grass reflected back –
in deep hues of red, yellow and orange –
lives full of intensity and a desire for uncertainty,
discomfort even, at times,

unstructured days when we ran hard through the world
before we went to sleep hard
with chests ebbing and flowing rapidly
in the sub-terrain.

Living

Blessed are those who ne'er let go
of life's ideals.

Blessed are those who pursue
life's dreams.

Blessed are those who can do this and still accept life
on its terms.

For these little ones life is not too strong,
and they sing, with the great heavenly wise –

"All the way to paradise is paradise."

Contemplation

In contemplation exists another world where I,
though alone at supper, am with a table full of guests;
Herman, Henry, Juan, William, Emily, Ernest (not Hemingway) –
they are all here, minds touching through metaphor:
the poetic cetology, the pond, *la llama viva del amor*,
the songs of innocence, the heather and the moor
and the memory of Elephant Island (as if I had been there before) –
all erasing the chasm of years.
I do not say I wish I had known them, for I do know them
here, here at this very table in the eternal now, feasting
on seal hooch and closer to one another
than William was to his wife, who lovingly once remarked
she had very little of his company because he was always in
Paradise.

Hunger

If my life were undomesticated
I would run wild through the haygrass fields
until my legs gave way to inertia and
I flopped down onto my belly rolling
until covered in dandelions.
Then I would get up and walk wag-tongued
to a rebel stream, lapping up the blue cool,
before settling 'neath a willow's shade.

This sometimes I would rather do
than always being let out at 7:00, 5:00 and 9:00,
my stomach filled at 8:00 and 4:00,
while the sound of a sit-com plays on the TV
and I lie passively on the couch, slipping
into hard-liquor sleep.

A Gift

We pulled ourselves up and over another
mound of jagged, slippery rocks, confident
the summit was near. Katahdin would be conquered,
we thought.
            But each time, through
the fog and horizontal rain,
our eyes raised, my companion
and I made out
another mound not far
away.

            The weather worsened.
Crag after crag,
we soon wearied, hands
cold, shriveled and
losing feeling. One
foot in this crevice,
the other in that,
then pull,
then re-position.
Katahdin seemed against us;
it was not the Nature
we were used to.

My companion cursed
the mountain while I talked
to myself, wondering
if my words would slur.
Then a wind gust
nearly knocked me
off balance

on a more
northerly
exposed rock,
the hood of my
raincoat
flying off and
flapping in
the wind.
      I reached
back and secured it,
and for another
mile we trudged over
the tablelands between
more mounds of rock,
our hearts rising and
leveling with the terrain,
passing the junction leading
to Thoreau Spring,
before finally reaching
the summit.

That day, at the mountain's base, we pondered our experience:
Does Nature have a nature? A character? An image of God marked
    upon it?
My sullen face looked at his as if in a mirror –
O Mother Nature! We have trekked safely through your home
    for so long, seeking peace and pleasure.
But you are not who we thought after all, neither good nor bad,
    or both, and unlike us, even lack the capacity to be so.
With sadness, yes, but with a quickening joy also, we have come to
    know it is our maker we have sought,
    and He,
    us.

Wild or Tame?

What reflects God more –
a forest wild or nature arranged,
one who's wild or one who's tame?

Is not wild to order
as sanguine is to melancholic –
two sides of the same beauty?

It seems right, then, that beauty
– and truth –
can be either wild or tame

and that tamed beauty
done right
can be lovely too.

It Was All a Blurrrrrrrrr

It was all a blurrrrrrrr
from the moment I threw my bottle down
'til I hit the floorrrrrrrrr.

   fists flailing lights
  shifting stools scattering
      cockroaches beer spattering glasses
   shattering adrenaline
        voices meaty
blurrrrrrrrred by the alcohol
    piercing vegan voices screaming
      blunted by the alcohol
     shuffling feet a roundhouse
                      and oh throbbing ribs
              oh
    knuckles head ducking sidekick to the knee
          buckling

It was all a blurrrrrrrr
from the moment I threw my bottle down
'til I hit the floorrrrrrrrr.

In the Park

It's a soft spring day, warm,
the sunshine breaking through the thin
icing of clouds. I sit under a gigantic oak tree
in the park, reading *The Selected Poems of
Wendell Berry*. A girl, somewhere in her twenties,
sits at a distance on one of those concrete park benches,
one leg dangling over the other, her foot shaking wildly,
wearing a turquoise sun-dress, looking down at an iPhone
between her long, slender fingers and occasionally, for
no apparent reason, darting her pony-tailed head to
one side like a bird, the same side where her white
purse sits on the concrete bench, its metal
gleaming in the sunlight, her movie-star
sunglasses gigantic on her face.

She's pretty, I think,
but she's not my type.

An Encounter

The Sunday school teacher spoke with a smile
as she spread her arms wide and exclaimed,
"We are all Christians!"

                      A boy on the
front row raised his hand: "I ain't a
Christian."

            The teacher looked worried, darting
her eyes. "Why do you say that?"
she asked. "We are all disciples of Jesus."

The boy lowered his chin and stammered, "But they ...
they just seem ... I mean, a Christian does not
like Jesus but a disciple of Jesus
does."

        The teacher stood still, her body
tense. Then the tenseness in her face
softened, as if an ocean tide had rolled
in and erased what had been there before.
A tear, which had grown out of the corner
of her eye, rolled down her cheek.

"Ain't I right?" the boy asked.

                      The teacher's
lips trembled. A holy silence engulfed
the room. The other children in this country
school sat in awe, as if beholding
Paw.

Pain and Beauty

Pain and beauty are bound,
like mother and son,
father and daughter,
lover and beloved.

In each great person's life,
great singer's voice
and great artist's work,
lies pain trans-

　formed.

So alas, sweet pain, come!
Tear the veil of this cocoon!
So that the heart might
take winged flight!

Age of Exploration

I wish I was living during the age of exploration
– not of space, but of Earth.
I would tread and sail upon every contour of its surface,
and when neither a land or seafaring route to traverse,
I would swing upon vines and leap among branches,
looking out upon virginal lakes and mountains,
every now and then shinnying down from the canopies
and bushwhacking my way to those lakes, skinny-
dipping in them and drinking their clear crystal draught,
all the while feeling, sensing
a mammoth of a beast – a mountain lion perhaps –
pulsating, eager
to jump out from the forbidden forest's fecund edge and
pounce on me.

Now I simply sit back and watch the TV
as NASA and the nightly news be my vicar.

Things Foreign

With what ease do Nature's beings
move through the world
until enter things foreign:
plastic from a six-pack,
monofilament line
– something to get entangled in.

Yet how amazingly adaptable is humankind,
in contrast, to things foreign.

Prayer upon a Wall

Once upon a time
in a playschool room
I saw a prayer upon a wall.
It was written with red Crayon
on big, white poster board.
It said:

Dear God, help me today
to be nice and to be kind
and to offer my friend something to eat
if he forgot his lunch.

In the front office
was another prayer upon a wall.
It was elegantly framed
and partly hidden by a plastic plant.
It said:

Lord, Almighty, and Everlasting Savior,
Deign to assist me
In being courteous and charitable
To those with whom I may
Have an encounter this day.

For Ezra

On a Sidewalk of the City

The apparition of these smokers outside corporate;
outcasts once incorporate.

From the Second Floor of the YMCA

The apparition of these bodies on treadmills;
hamsters on wheels.

Wrapper in the Wild

I abhor a wrapper in the wild.
Even though God, who
made the wild,
made us
and we, the wrapper,
'tis a relative too distant.
In the city it is forgivable,
it's being flung on the ground.
But no one should throw a wrapper down
in the wild.

Upon Meeting a Certain Woman

A fine eccentricity there was about her
– in the refreshing sense,

lacking in trite chatter
and endowed with a Shakespearean poetic
that was fact of matter,

a personality agreeable,
open, willing
and so casually adventurous,

in short, a romantic underneath her
mathematical skin.

The Place We Grew Up In

As I watched the waning, orange moon rising,
I stretched out my hands and beheld a thought:
When I leave this Earth will I ever miss it?
Not the people I mean (they will always be with me),
but the things of this Earth.

Aren't this place and the things of it, after all,
a part of our history, our childhood, our growing up,
making us who we are
and who we're going to be?

Surely, I will miss these and, missing them,
desire to come back.
But even then,
what if, in a time to come, the Earth is no more?

It would seem strange if we could not visit again
the place we grew up in.

Gibberish

"Sush ki fompo croush," he said.

The girl behind the fast-food
counter ignored him, continuing
to count the money and placing it
into an imaginary pouch.

Another customer walked in
from the noisy street and asked,
"Foar kant sheed tor foosh?"

The girl pointed to the restroom
door and exclaimed, *"Majoak
palot ta freesh!"*

                The two
customers briefly glanced at each
other, one *afroompt* and the
other *afaloompic.*

III

The mountains are calling, and I must go.

– John Muir, in a letter to Sarah Muir Galloway

I began walking down one of the wheel paths, two flies now cutting in and out around my head and tall, sandpaper-like weeds sticking to my bare arms. I was beginning to break a sweat. As I walked on, I awakened a bug in the undergrowth on my left, and it began making a burning, stinging sound, piercing the eerie quietness and startling me for a moment. I stepped over small muddy puddles here and there, the faint road undulating along uneven ground. In one spot, vines had begun to stretch across the road on both sides, like fingers striving to connect with one another. Up ahead in the distance, I saw an abandoned cabin, which nature was swallowing in its grip. I heard the notes of a yellow-throated warbler nearby, somewhere along the edge of the woods. The day being windless, the bird's salutary melody punctuated the air. I continued toward the cabin, the thick weeds enclosing my legs and lone mosquitoes biting here and there at my neck and arms. It was getting close to dusk, and as the sun began to sink into the reddening sky the forest cast a growing shadow upon the land. I knew once the sun set, the darkness of the forest and all the mosquitoes would come alive, haunting any human soul stranded in it. I knew I needed to get out of the woods and back to the main road before the sun set entirely behind the mountains. So, turning around, I walked quickly through the undergrowth, back toward the car. The wild, I thought, can be a dangerous place, yet a magical and mystical one too. It is, after all, where true life resides. As I looked westward, the setting sun's light stubbornly beamed forth its rays into my face, making one final prolonged protest before plummeting to its demise.

I Once Met a Soul

I

I once met a soul as young as mine
but thirty years older in time,
and thought, if she were thirty years younger
I would have fallen in love:
soul mates, meant for communion
in another world.

II

I once met a soul as old as mine
but thirty years younger in time,
and thought, if she were thirty years older
I would have fallen in love:
soul mates, meant for communion
in another world.

To My Love

I have watched you long
days from the hillside shade,
you glistening white
in the golden field.
And when the time was right
I leapt lion-footed from the shadows
into the rejoicing light.

The Garbage Man

When I was a child my mama always warned me that if I didn't do well in school and apply myself I would grow up to be
    a garbage man.

When I got older my philosophy professor told us everybody is equal, that a doctor or lawyer or businessman is no better than
    a garbage man.

Today the preacher told us when he walked to the mailbox the other day the garbage man smiled at him and asked how his day was going – and how, in this act of kindness, the garbage man had reflected the love of Jesus more than even he had that day, and therefore that we should all strive to be like
    the garbage man.

Now I'm starting to question what my mama told me.

Mystery

Skeptics siphon mystery out –
denying what is,
by heart, mysterious.

For one should not put life in a box
but put the box into life,
then throw it out the wide, western window
into the warm, easterly wind
and then, turn around, and be ready for
surprise.

Agnosticism

The best argument against agnosticism
is man fully alive – or man fully dead,
whipped by the weight of materialism,
having lived out the philosophy of said.

The Final Hour

After I died I found myself amid rows.
Others were there too and, like me,
were waiting, behind me,
some kneeling, some sitting.
I had been there awhile and, though the place was quiet,
my soul was loud.

*You made us for yourself, O Lord,
and our hearts find no peace until they rest in you*

I looked at my watch.
It had stopped at three o'clock,
though I could not tell whether in the morning or afternoon.
A woman had gone in before me.
I heard the hollow sound of high heels and saw a glimpse
of her strong calf muscles as she closed the regal door
behind her.

*Grace builds upon nature without destroying it
and glory, without obliterating, perfects*

My palms were sweaty.
I had been through this five hundred and thirty-nine times,
to be infinitely exact.
One would have thought I could not keep promises,
but this, this,
in a mysterious way,
this making of mistakes and coming back
had seemed to enable me to keep my promise.

I, a sinner, take you to be my spouse.

I promise to be true to you

But now it was the final hour.
Why should it be different than before?
I will say another prayer, I thought,
then realized
it was too late for that –
I heard the knob turn and the heavy door swung
open. The woman in high heels walked out with a glow
transcending the makeup she wore.
It was now my turn to enter.

*Father, forgive me,
for I am a sinner*

Freedom

It is a good thing, in the presence of another
and the world at large,
to be able to speak one's mind freely
and to be able to be wrong without ramification

– but not without reciprocation –

for certainly one has an obligation
not to take lightly this allowance
and to always be open to truth
and to continuous revision.

When I Soared Above the Clouds

When I soared above the clouds in a jumbo jet plane,
seeing the billows of white, like cotton balls of
mountains and palaces as far as eye could see,
I thought of the choleric apostle stepping onto Galilee
and how, if I were to step out onto that cotton,
reality would set in.

But what if my faith became mustard-seed sized,
a downsized faith up-sized?
What if what appears to be another kingdom really is?
Then, I just might be able to move those mountains
of cotton balls so as to lay a foundation on which to build
a tender palace of my own.

What the Sea Saw

The celestial show-shimmering sphere
shone across the sky,
sweeping away the star shine.

Only me it seemed to see,
only it I,
drawing me ever nearer, pulling me,

me like tide, gently grabbing me by my blood-stained tie,
drawing me up, up, up toward its christening light
and I

pulling back, uncertain, and it not letting go.
I howled at it, howled loudly,
and suddenly the night was wild and lyrical,

like trombones hooting amid saxophones whining,
like phantasmal shadows dancing upon abysmal waters blackened.
Out of nowhere, somewhere, I could hear a faint

whirring. It grew louder and louder,
and still louder,
until it multiplied all around me.

Though frightened, I hesitated no more,
and blinded by the white,
floating, as it were, above the wafer-shaped sphere,

I could see,
I could see,
what the sea saw!

Love in the Wild

If I were a weed
I would grow in the wild,
in a field far and wide,
beside a yellow tulip.
And each night
I would wrap myself gently a-
round this fair flowering maiden
swaying to the rhythm of katydids,
and kiss her deferring petals
'til dawn.

Like unto These

Like a front kick that reaches as high as the belt,
like a pizza whose cheese hasn't had time to melt,
like a fiddle's A-string plucked and ringing out flat,
like a developer's housing plan that looks just pat

– who is it? I ask. Who is like unto these?

Like a snowcapped mountain against a glass-blue sky,
like a novel or musical composition beyond well nigh,
like a painted tree's deciduous leaves each displaying veins,
like a cheetah's chasing down prey and ingesting the gains

– who is it? I ask. Who will be like unto these?

Naming Things

As of late, I have gotten into the habit of naming things,
random things –
the type of grass in my yard,
the kinds of weeds, bushes and trees growing
at the woods edge just across the street.

Perhaps it is because they are increasingly
decreasing that I am not content anymore
with just calling it all
flora.

You and I
and even Kai Hynson and Riley Wysor, too,
tend to give these
a vague look.

But this dullness of sight is
dull.

Improv

A horse jumped over the barnyard fence!
Yes, and the fence jumped over the horse when the tornado hit!
Yes, and the tornado shook up all the chickens like dice!
Yes, and the dice were thrown!
Yes, and the chickens landed in the town!
Yes, to lay eggs for the starving people ravished by the tornado!
Yes, mistakes are a gift!
Yes, like improv!
Yes, in a way, life should be lived like improv.

Love's Approach

Love came so quietly I did not notice its approach;
the heart was high in the mast
but had been on the lookout for something else
as the approach came from another
angle.

I did not know what I had been on the lookout for;
only the inner soul knew
that in her was everything I thought I ever wanted
and everything I never knew I ever
needed.

Holiness

I had always assumed holiness would shout
its presence from the rooftops,
unique as it is among the masses.

Yet I wonder if I would even recognize it,
should its presence retain no trace of Gabriel's wings,
only the sound of daily things?

Or if it would rub me the wrong way,
and I in time would come to know it,
having been changed by it?

Or if I would ever come to know it,
though it were right in front of me all the time,
like God?

Anticipation

The wind kissed me tenderly
on the lips
as deep blue clouds trudged easterly

Birds gossiped excitedly
in the bright green trees

There was the sound of elves
throwing strikes and spares
behind the horizon

Then the smell of wet aroma
and the pounding of a strike
and the thick drops
and gusts of horns and clashing cymbals
and then
              the anticipation

                        burst

then flat-lined
causing a pall
to fall
over all
of nature

Before Dusk

From my kitchen window each day
at nearly 7:45 on the dot,
just before dusk,
a couple walks by along the unpaved road,
hand in hand,
sometimes talking, often laughing
and swinging each other's arms
with abandon.

There is something about the routine of it,
the order of it,
in an irregular world.

Today I didn't see the couple;
I wondered if something had happened.
I looked down at my iPhone,
seeing the number from which my sister had called,
and as I am about to call her back,
realize
that one day this ordered sequence of meaning
will be no more –
a time once was,
a black & white photograph
I had forgotten to take
and had forgotten I had forgotten

until, like today, something happens,
like the couple's not passing by
hand in hand
along the unpaved road, at the wild woods edge,

at nearly 7:45 on the dot,
making me realize the beauty of routine –
even my own routine
of standing in the kitchen
just before dusk –
while it lasts,
while there is still   daylight.

Mystical Union

100,000,000,000 + 3 = 1

Compatibility

An orange is not compatible with pizza,
but pineapple is.
Strawberries go with kiwi,
but not cucumbers and Granny Smith apples,
though their color is the same.

Tomatoes and bananas
– two fruits –
do not mix.
But raisins go with lettuce,
though one is fruit and the other vegetable.

Yet even raisins
would never be as good with lettuce
without a vinaigrette,
which binds the two together,
like holy matrimony.

Balance Sheets

Gerry

Assets

full-time job
own home
no car payment
pet bird
single
master's degree
lover of truth and others

Liabilities

student loans
mortgage
frequent car repairs
no hairy friend
suffering

Equity

pearl of great price

Darryl

Assets

part-time job
rent apartment
new car
pet dog
married
diploma
lover of deceit

Liabilities

no degree
no home equity
car payment
pet care
suffering

Equity

nothing

Shadows

One soul flickered white amidst a buzzing fly,
casting its sultry form upon a grassy field.

Another soul flickered yellow before an owl's espy,
casting its wintry form upon a darkened hill.

Ah, but for the mercy of the abstract eye,
how the shadows obscure the flame!

Bright-eyed and Young

God is a great lover! a great adventurer!
a wild one at heart with a daring spark!

He ain't Santa Claus, 'ole Saint Nick!
well, he's that too! but that's not all –

Yes, God is bright-eyed and young!
very young! younger than us all!

If we age in God's grace we grow younger,
not older, with each passing year –

More up for a vigorous swim in the moonlight
than a bedside read in the lamplight!

First and Last Things

To want to reform the world,
go down in history,
be famous,
be original

– so often desires
the artificial.

But the real?

If you're serious about
the first and the last,
then first,
go to your room,
shut the door
and do nothing
except listen,

and last,
take action
if you're beckoned
and if you're still serious about
the first and last things.

When I Arrived in Heaven

When I arrived in heaven I was surprised,
not that I had arrived (well, that too) –
but I was surprised at all the work going on.
I had always heard that heaven was a place
of rest and peace.

At the moment I arrived, a teacher welcomed me warmly.
I asked her, "Where is your resting place?"
"Here we do not rest," she replied.
"If you had gone south, where it is cooler,
much cooler, you would have had a resting place."

I was startled at her response
and wondered whether I was in the right place.
She must have read my mind:
"Oh, this is where you want to be alright," she said.
"There is no better place."

"Oh," I murmured, in astonishment.
"Yes," she continued. "Here we work to find rest and peace,
just like on earth, if you had found your niche."
"I guess I didn't find my niche, then.
Work for me there was very tiring."

"That's okay," she said.
"We'll put you to work now,
doing what you always wanted to do."
"And what is that?" I asked.
"Building things," she replied.

"Yes, you're right, I always did like that.
Circumstance just didn't allow for it."
"Right, and that's the way it was supposed to be,
back on earth. Things were different there.
You'll come to understand."

"See those people over there?" she asked.
"Yes, what is it they are building?"
"A castle for others to live in."
"It looks beautiful," I said.
"That's because they have eternity to build it, and to build it right."

"And see those people over there?"
"Yes, it appears they're cooking something.
It smells good, like … well, like this place."
"Yes, their gift was cooking, and they love to cook
for all the builders living in that castle over there."

It was then that I thought I recognized a man
standing amidst the builders, though with a clean-shaven face.
"I'm going to take you over there now," she said,
her eyes radiant. "And they already love you
and have been expecting you."

"Sure," I replied, my heart now burning.
"I better be on my way now," she said. "I'll see you later."
Then she vanished, leaving me transfixed upon him
and the infinite intricacies of the castle
and how they almost seemed to be one and the same.

About the Author

Bart Price was born in Nashville, Tennessee, in 1975 and grew up mostly in a rural area east of the city. In 1998, he earned a bachelor's degree in English from Cumberland University. While there, he served as editor of the university's newspaper, *The Phoenix Review*, and founded the university's literary magazine, *The Roving Eye*. Also, while pursuing his bachelor's, he completed an internship at Thomas Nelson Publishers, Inc. in Nashville, editing fiction and non-fiction books. After graduation, Bart worked as a city and county government reporter and occasional columnist for *The Lebanon Democrat* newspaper in Lebanon, Tennessee. While there, he also wrote for the city's local magazine, *Our Home*. Later, he moved to St. Augustine, Florida, where he took a position as police and legal reporter for *The St. Augustine Record* newspaper. While at the newspaper, he earned two awards from Florida Press Club's Excellence in Journalism, one in the category of In-Depth News Writing and the other in Environmental Writing. After leaving the news business to pursue a career in finance, he occasionally wrote freelance articles for *The National Catholic Register*. In 2012, he had three poems published in the second volume of *Open Mic Jacksonville, Vol. II*, a poetry and short story collection featuring authors of northeast Florida. Currently, Bart is a manager in the Merrill Lynch division of Bank of America and lives in St. Augustine.

Aside from work and writing poetry, Bart enjoys challenging adventures. In the summer of 2011, he hiked Maine's 100-Mile Wilderness and climbed Mt. Katahdin. In 2012, he hiked part of California's John Muir Trail, which stretches approximately 218 miles from Yosemite National Park to Mt. Whitney. Bart also composes music, plays guitar and sings. In 2006, he and four musicians released an album entitled *Miles to Go*, which comprises music set to Scripture psalms. Like much of his poetry, the album reflects a synthesis of the natural and the spiritual. As such, the musical arrangements combine the sounds of acoustic instruments with the eternal truths of the lyrics. One day, if time permits, Bart would like to publish a sheet music collection of songs he has written over the years, as well as record another album. In the meantime, he is planning to begin work on a second volume of poetry.

www.ingramcontent.com/pod-product-compliance
Lightning Source LLC
Chambersburg PA
CBHW030636150426
42811CB00077B/2179/J